FASHION AND *Color*

Mary Garthe

First published in the United States of America by:
Rockport Publishers, Inc.
146 Granite Street, Rockport, Massachusetts 01966-1299
Telephone: (508) 546-9590
Fax: (508) 546-7141

Distributed to the book trade and art trade in the United States by:
North Light, an imprint of
F & W Publications
1507 Dana Avenue, Cincinnati, Ohio 45207
Telephone: (513) 531-2222

First Published in Singapore by Rockport Publishers for:
Page One—The Bookshop Pte Ltd
Blk 4, Pasir Panjang Road
#08-33 Alexandra Distripark
Singapore 0511
Telephone: (65) 273-0128
Fax: (65) 273-0042

Published and distributed in Thailand by:
Asia Books Co., Ltd.
5 Sukhumvit Soi 61
P.O. Box 40
Bangkok 10110, Thailand
Telephone: (662) 391-2680, 391-0590
Fax: 381-1621, 391-2277

Other Distribution by:
Rockport Publishers, Inc.
Rockport, Massachusetts 01966-1299

ISBN 1-56496-174-5

10 9 8 7 6 5 4 3 2 1

Editor: Shawna Mullen
Art Direction & Design: Laura Herrmann Design
Cover Illustration/Fashion Illustrations: Michael Lenn
Cover Calligraphy: H. A. Lind
Photographer: John Kane
Stylist: Mary Garthe
Hair and Make-up: Christine Clemente

Manufactured in Singapore by Regent Production Services Pte. Ltd.

FASHION AND *Color*

Mary Garthe

ROCKPORT PUBLISHERS

Rockport Publishers, *Rockport, Massachusetts*

Acknowledgments

Like any project of this nature, this book is not specifically the work of a single person: it could only have attained its current level of polish with the enthusiasm and professionalism of my colleagues John Kane and Misha Lenn.

Special thanks are due to Rockport Publishers for believing in me and for giving me the opportunity to develop this book, and especially for the editorial direction of Shawna Mullen. My thanks to the many fine stores—and especially to Jacqueline Budd from Bloomingdales—galleries, and designers, who so graciously loaned the fashions featured in the book. My thanks also to Jo Somers, Dalarna and Shawna of *Copley Seven;* to Maggie, Liz, Juenelle, and Christine of *Maggie, Inc.;* to Katrice and Marlana; and to Michael Mekan of *Silver Sun Studios.* Thanks go to Christine Clemente, who demonstrated—through the magic of her colors and brushes—that makeup is a form of art; to Laura Herrmann for her skill and imagination in the art direction of the book; and to Jay Calderin and Catharine Arnston for invaluable artistic and literary assistance.

I am grateful to the Belcher family, who graciously opened their home to me during the initial stages of this book, and to my children and the many friends who took an interest in my work and continually encouraged it. To all of these people I owe the ultimate success of this book.

—Mary Garthe

Table of Contents

Introduction

Most who undertake the interpretation of color rely solely on the very traditional equations between primary, secondary, and tertiary colors and their many hues. Color is infinitely more complex and challenging when the human element is factored in.

Color's voice speaks of cultural influences, as well as mood and emotional motivation, in a language particular to the person using it. Human response to history and to the environment is the heart of the decision-making process. Personal associations explain the world's many and varied perceptions of color. The endless combinations of who, what, where, why, when, and how become a colorful celebration of diversity and individuality simultaneously.

The nature of fashion presents additional issues that must be addressed, allowing for even greater possibilities. This is at the very core of an art form—fashion—that redefines and recreates itself every season. The selection of color for fashion involves three areas: prediction, application and description.

The first, **prediction,** means forecasting: the study of color trends, past and present. It may also include the environment in which the color will be applied and an understanding of the target consumer.

Application is the means of communicating a message. If a bright, sunny yellow is the color of choice, a decision must then be made: will it be used as the foundation for a garment or as an accent? Both choices give the color great importance, but each relays a uniquely different message.

Description. What's in a name? Red may be called cherry, tomato, brick, barn, claret, crimson, scarlet, ruby, or rose. This is true of any of the fundamental colors. Every designer approaches color from their own perspective, and each design and fabrication evokes a different response. They can't all be just plain red, what would be the fun of that?

Mavericks don't follow trends, they create new ones through the innovative nature of their rebellion. A designer may choose a color and then apply it in ways contrary to popular expectations. Today's international marketplace allows for haute couture, deconstruction, reconstruction, and mass-produced basics—to mention only a few. The size and scope of any faction of the fashion industry may vary, but the availability of choice is the key. Some of the most successful statements are those made from a personal point of view. When someone finds a color story that best illustrates the image they are trying to project, it becomes their safety net. With that security in place, they are then free to experiment with passing fads.

The points touched upon in this book are a sampling of the rich supply of inspiration and raw materials the world landscape provides. The fashion world is now influenced from many directions. The future lies in establishing a strong, basic appreciation for color theory, then applying it to the adventure of understanding and interpreting color each time.

Fashion and Color can be used as a starting point for investigating the many possible applications of color in fashion. In these pages, color combinations, effective color messages, and creative uses of color are all explored within the context of culture, historical reference, environmental factors, emotional assignments to color, and, most importantly, a strong regard for style.

Jay Calderin
Publisher/Editor-In-Chief
Maverick Magazine

The Color Wheel

Color Schemes

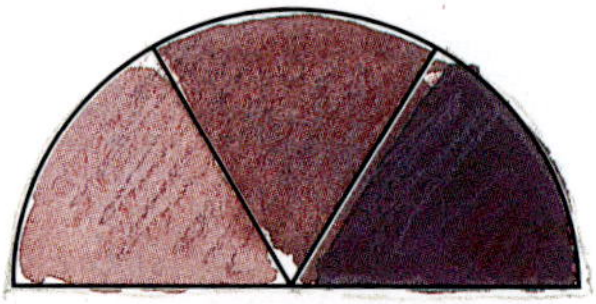

Monochromatic

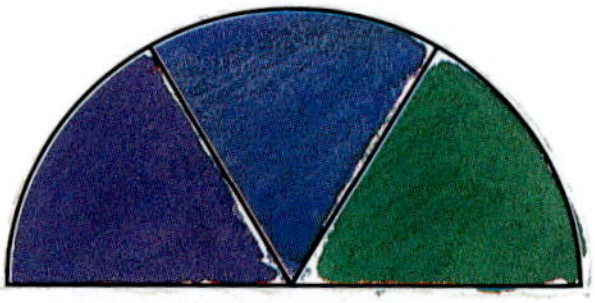

Analogous

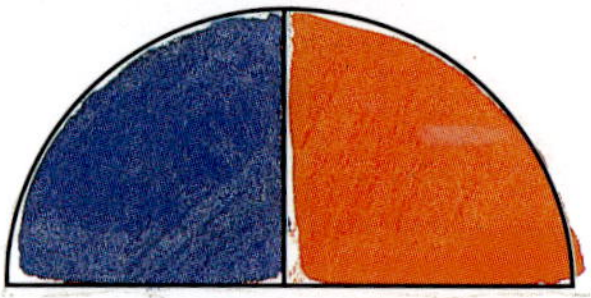

Complementary

Split-Complementary

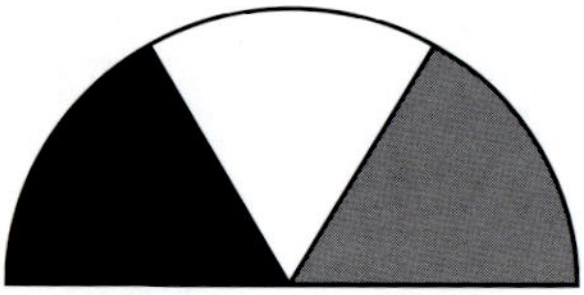

Achromatic

The Color Wheel

Sir Isaac Newton designed the first color circle. This became the color wheel; the map that we use today to predict a color's appearance. A color's hue and intensity can be determined according to its coordinates on the wheel, thus the wheel acts as a color ordering system that helps us mix or match colors.

The twelve segments of the color wheel consist of primary, secondary, and tertiary hues and their specific tints and shades. Starting with red at the top, the primary hues of red, yellow, and blue form an equilateral triangle within the wheel. The three secondary hues, orange, violet, and green, stand between the primary hues and form another triangle. Finally, red orange, yellow orange, yellow green, blue green, blue violet, and red violet, all combinations of a primary and secondary hue, form the six tertiary hues. This arrangement gives visual order to the sequence of color balance and harmony.

Because the color wheel arranges color systematically, it is invaluable to the designer seeking to develop a specific color scheme. For the purposes of this book, five color schemes are discussed: monochromatic, analogous, achromatic, complementary, and split-complementary.

Monochromatic schemes consist of any shade or tint of a single color. Analogous schemes incorporate any shade, tint or tone of colors that are adjacent to each other on the wheel. Achromatic schemes are considered colorless because they contain only blacks, whites, and grays. Complementary schemes combine shades or tones of a color and the hue found opposite on the color wheel, for example, yellow and violet. Split-complementary schemes combine a single color with the colors adjacent to its complement on the color wheel.

Whether you are building a wardrobe, designing a line of clothing, or simply choosing an ensemble, this valuable color guide will help identify color combinations that are harmonious and beautiful.

How to Use This Book

The colors we choose to surround ourselves with communicate much about our way of life, our culture, and our beliefs, perceptions, and inner feelings. To articulate this "visual message", we add form and texture to the mix. And the voice of color speaks perhaps the loudest in individual clothing choices. A wardrobe that lacks a balance of color sends an incomplete message.

Color's quiet impact comes from the fact that it is both decorative and evocative: blue is "cool," red is "warm," and light and dark refer not only to the amount of white or black a color contains, but also to moods those colors suggest.

This book introduces the language of color in terms of clothing. Getting dressed is an an age old ritual, so why is it still so difficult? Why do so many of us have closets stuffed full of clothing, yet feel we have nothing to wear? By presenting visual examples of how color combinations work, the pages that follow try to offer some practical answers.

Most of us already have favorite colors or favorite color combinations. We also tend to wear limited palettes—the same four or five hues over and over again. To encourage experimentation, each chapter in this book is an at-a-glance guide to "what works with what." Chapters follow the sequence of the color wheel, while supporting photos and illustrations present variations on color messages. Some combinations are monochromatic, others cover a vivid spectrum. Color terms such as saturated, contrasting, accent, and tone-on-tone are defined with actual ensembles. All of the clothing is carefully selected for timeless silhouettes that avoid the ebb and flow of trendiness and high fashion. Some combinations show contrast, some have distinct cultural messages.

The range of each featured color is explored in sections that demonstrate how the same hue can move from day to evening wear. Finally, a sampling of fabric swatches reveals how texture influences and changes the message of color.

It is our hope that *Fashion and Color* will inspire you to add new hues to your wardrobe, to discover new shades of colors you once thought were unflattering, and to feel that trying on a new color doesn't have to be an alarming experience.

Fashion and Color Palette

Red

Red

Simply wearing red is an act of confidence that commands attention.

From bright RED to deep crimson to rose madder, red evokes strong images: It symbolizes the pulse of life, passion, elation, and energy. Red advances visually, a property that makes it seem closer to the viewer than another color the same distance away, and one that may account for red's seductive reputation. In Chinese culture, red (the symbol of active force), not white, is the counterpoint to black (the symbol of passive force). When worn alone, red is hot, passionate and powerful. When subdued by the addition black or white, as in burgundy or dark pink shades, red retains its impact, but takes on an air of mystery—as something veiled or just under the surface.

Saturated

Here, the shine of polished leather adds depth and boosts the intensity of saturated red, exalting the ordinary short boot to the realm of the unusual. Saturated red accessories can become the punctuation marks in an otherwise sober or serious outfit.

Analogous

Red becomes sporty in combination with violet and stripes. Because of the fundamental strength of red, it is easy to play other colors against it. Conversely, though red is always vigorous, it can almost work as a neutral, since it combines well with a surprising variety of colors.

Contrasting

Red and red orange are hot against the contrast of cool blue denim. The effect is youthful and energetic. Dark blues and greens as a backdrop to red are real cornerstones of fashion—turning up in everything from classic, tartan plaids to young, spirited designs for sportswear.

Combining Red

RED combines well with itself and with other warm colors: persimmon and ox blood, orange and lacquer red, etc. Since there are almost as many versions of red as there are colors to mix it with,

ENERGETIC *Red with orange is strong and distinctive. This combination is often used in high fashion, but can also express good humor and fun.*

SUBDUED *Accessorizing magenta with brown subdues the red hues and adds sophistication: This pairing is especially effective when used with matte fabrics or tweeds.*

pay attention to the underlying hue of red when coordinating it in an ensemble. Some reds, such as crimson and watermelon, have a strong blue element that helps them mix well with cool colors. Others veer toward yellow and orange, and can be exploited to create hot, brilliant combinations. The charm and drama of using red is the freedom it offers, in combinations of boldness or beauty.

VIVID *The sharp contrast of red against bright yellow is bold. These strong colors are best worn in summer or in tropical climates, where they will not pale in bright light.*

SPICY *Crisp, spicy red with a pinker shade of medium salmon red is interesting and contemporary.*

COOLED *The contrast of a blue red with moss green combines the quiet of nature with the pop of a bright tone. The colors are pulled back in this ensemble, to prevent them from creating a hard edge.*

URBAN *Again, a subdued color (aubergine) emphasizes the brighter color, red, to create a rich and urban combination.*

Day Color

RED is versatile; although a wide spectrum of colors are called red, most are appropriate for wear during the day. Season, climate, and fabric weight dictate the use of red in a design much more than the time of day the outfit will be worn.

Pale reds are best interpreted using chiffon, sheer linen or silk, which are fabrics that complement the lightest colors. As the amount of saturated color increases, so too can the weight of the fabric.

Evening Color

Bold, fire engine RED, is often seen in dramatic dinner suits or evening dresses. The power of this color must be equalized by the strength of the garment design, or the ensemble's impact becomes oddly off-balance.

When red becomes even deeper, its effect grows sultry. Deep red colors such as cinnabar are not as aggressive as truer, saturated reds. Instead, they read as exotic and intriguing. Deep red is a complex color with both cool and warm aspects. Artificial light will bring out its warmth, while sunlight will make it appear more violet.

Red Textiles

Color is one of the most significant aspects in fabric, and often the determining factor for purchasing, therefore, the dyes or pigments must be carefully chosen for compatibility with the fiber. Applying the color so that it penetrates and holds in the fiber is very complicated. Azoic dyes, used to produce bright REDs, were developed in the 1880s in England. The oldest azoic dyes are *Para red* and *Naphthylamine Bordeaux.* Prior to the invention of azoic dyes, red dyes came from the root of the madder plant, from the Brazilwood tree and the powder from ground shells of the insect *kermes.*

Orange

Orange

Orange is a powerful and often misunderstood color.

Many people feel they cannot wear ORANGE at all. This is not true. Versatile orange ranges from the palest hue of flattering peach to electric, modern shades at full saturation, to rich, subdued earth tones. Orange in fashion can be used to evoke anything from the hard-edged, urban image of traffic cones and construction sites, to the tropical stillness of citrus groves and sunsets. The key to wearing orange successfully—either alone or in combination—is in carefully matching the shade you choose to the style you seek to project.

contrasting

We traditionally think of yellow-green and orange combinations as tropical. However, in cooler climates, or worn as an accessory to an outfit, yellow-green makes an orange scheme fresh, young, and trendy.

Analogous

In fashion, unsaturated orange shaded to brown-orange conveys a message of reliability and reserve. Here, adding strands of warm red and yellow beads to the deep shade of the dress creates an analogous color combination that is sophisticated without being cold.

Monochromatic

The orange coat commands attention, so it becomes necessary to subdue it with a dull color to create a sense of harmony and balance. Simply shading orange to brown in the shoes and hose anchors the boldness of the coat.

combining orange

ORANGE is worn most easily in combination with its tints and shades, or with its complements. Adding a second color to orange in an outfit modifies the strong message (*look at me*) pure

BRIGHT *Yellow-green with yellow-orange, although difficult for most women to wear, conveys a fresh bright quality.*

RICH *Subdued moss green and rust orange are rich and handsome for a fall and winter wardrobe.*

orange conveys. Pale or dull colors worn with orange subdue it, and can make it sophisticated and elegant. Bright or complementary hues enhance orange, and amplify its energy and brilliance. In short, the same orange scheme can be modified to suit a variety of tastes and personalities, simply through the addition of a second color.

PALE *Pale taupe with pale orange is quiet and elegant. This combination is especially flattering to gray hair color.*

SOFT *Blue and orange colors complement each other, but are best worn together when one color is at a lower intensity than the other.*

WARM *Red tones down the brightness of orange and makes it warmer, sending a message of fun and vitality about the wearer.*

CLASSIC *A classic combination, deep blue with brown orange is elegant in the city, but also works well in "country" styles, like handknit sweaters.*

Day Color

In its palest form ORANGE is almost a transparent blush. Pale orange tones work well under office lights, shedding a flattering peach light on skin tones. A slightly more saturated shade of orange works best in bright, daylight environments, since the stronger shade doesn't wash out in the strong light. Depending on the fabric, deeper shades of rust and brown can make orange conservative and businesslike, or warm and rustic.

Evening Color

Unsaturated ORANGE shaded to brown is traditionally considered dowdy. It becomes surprisingly elegant for evening if worn in velvet or taffeta fabrics. Burnt orange or burnt sienna is especially beautiful against dark skin tones, and for evening wear in silk or wool jersey fabrics.

Orange Textiles

Texture and fabric weight have a profound effect on color. The same ORANGE dye applied to linen, wool, and velvet will create three distinct hues. The palest orange hues work best in mid-weight fabrics such as linens, silks, and cashmeres. As orange intensifies in hue it becomes more commanding, and is best worn in matt fabrics to control its vitality.

Yellow

Yellow

Bold and electric, yellow stands out.

Americans use YELLOW in outerwear for safety, while in other parts of the world, yellow is considered more feminine than pink. Traditionally associated with the sun, yellow has a basic, almost primitive appeal. It remains a *sacred* color in many cultures, especially in the Orient. Worn with white or off-white, yellow glows. But be careful when pairing yellow with lavender or cool, pale blues, if either is too pale the combination will take on a grayish cast.

Yellow speaks to us of eternal summer when combined with white in a crisp gingham dress. It becomes sophisticated and mysterious subdued to the mellow tones of amber in a dress of silk organza.

complementary

Bright yellow and bright lilac are refreshing and sporty. This combination evokes thoughts of spring and is excellent when worn for casual wear. The transparency of yellow gives the ensemble a bright, modern look.

split-complementary

Yellow paired with pink can appear overly sweet. By adding other colors to the scheme, and deepening pink to a jewel tone of fuchsia, the mix becomes dramatic and even more bold. This vivid combination is bright and alive and takes yellow to the next dimension.

Primary Accents

Yellow is the most luminous primary color, and is next to white in its level of brightness. For this reason, it is especially dramatic with black. Often used in ethnic schemes, yellow and black lose their hard edge with the addition of vivid primary colors.

Combining Yellow

Because of its visibility, YELLOW is most often associated with outerwear—the dash of a bright yellow raincoat or shiny yellow boots. Recently, yellow has become popular for more than just

SHEER *The light textures of cotton and linen add interest to pale, clear yellow over a yellow-green dress.*

SUBDUED *Adding dark green subdues yellow and gives the yellow in the sweater a radiant effect.*

jackets and golfing trousers. Pure, bright yellow is cool, verging on sharp in its most saturated form. Deeper yellows, based in ochre, are warm and near golden. Cool yellows can be mixed with colors from either side of the color wheel; greens, or warmer yellows and reds. Warm yellows combine best with cool, neutral colors such as light gray or brown, and pale green or lavender.

WARM *The yellow-orange shirt and trousers are pulled together by the addition of the warm-toned yellow jacket in the same value.*

QUIET *Wear gray with medium yellow and the combination results in an interesting balance of quiet and bright.*

HOT *This splendid combination of yellow intensified with red is beautiful on dark skin tones, and translates well into many fabrics.*

BRIGHT *Yellow and blue are combined for a strong and energetic statement. The warmth of the yellow sweater brings brightness to the deep blue-violet trouser. Adding a deeper blue belt pulls the outfit together.*

Day Color

When worn in the daytime, the palest shade of YELLOW appears cream. A slightly darker shade of yellow is frequently paired with green, and other sympathetic, yellow-based colors, for daywear. Stripes, checks or floral prints often include yellow because of its ability to reflect light and act as a canvas. From butter to banana yellow, one tends to see yellow used in lighter fabrics that are often worn in warmer climates. In gabardine, wool jersey, and more substantial fabrics, deeper yellows such as saffron and amber work well.

Evening Color

YELLOW moves from its happy state to a more exotic sensibility as it approaches evening. Silk, velvet and taffeta are all found in royal shades of yellow-gold and are best worn for drama and the spotlight. Yellow is powerful enough to offset many of the duller neutrals; even a small amount of yellow gives zest to an entire scheme.

Yellow Textiles

The American market loves bright colors, and YELLOW translates well in the synthetic fabrics that create new expressions of a color. Never purchased in quantity, like black, designers use yellow as a brush stroke of color in a collection. Always popular in rainwear, as in the classic slicker, yellow has also been important for jacquards, activewear, and accessories.

Yellow-green

Yellow-green

YELLOW-GREEN is acidic and pert; it has the bite of citrus but the familiar comfort of green grass. Worn in an ensemble, it can be unpredictable or fresh as the spring. Lighting strongly affects the impact of this color, as does pairing it with other colors. It can appear exotic and tropical or unconventional and playful, depending on how it is partnered. When worn alone, it is a visual wake-up, a sensory bite of an unripe green apple. Such is the spirit of yellow-green.

Alive and alert is the message of yellow-green.

Split-Complement & Black

Though yellow-green is often associated with springtime, it can carry off combinations with stronger colors. It is striking coupled with red-violet, its complement. The vivid hues of a red hat and black sweater intensify the yellow-green of this jacket.

Analogous

Yellow-green actually contains a lot of blue, which makes it a more stable hue than pure yellow. While yellow-green is, technically speaking, too far away from blue-violet to be called analogous, this cool combination shares an underlying element of blue that unifies it and gives it the balance of an analogous combination.

Complementary

The subdued red and yellow-green in these sweaters is united by adding a silk scarf of the same value. The pairing works because each color is made up of both a warm and a cool tone.

combining yellow-green

The nineties herald the return of YELLOW-GREEN in fashion; a reflection of our need to be in harmony with nature. Not since 1945, when khaki and olive drab

FRESH *White added to yellow-green gives the combination a degree of brilliance and is fresh and young for spring.*

SPORTY *Yellow-green offset with blue is sporty and sophisticated. The blue has been subdued with black to tone it down for a more refined mood.*

were prevalent, has this difficult color emerged on the fashion landscape. Currently, the yellow-green of fashion is less brown and more saturated. It works best with medium bright colors, and also pairs well with pastels. Yellow-green brings a fresh appearance to an ensemble, but be careful of wearing it near the face; certain shades can cast an unflattering light.

TROPICAL *Pink and yellow-green, colorful and upbeat, are cool and feminine in light, summer-weight fabrics.*

NATURAL *The underlying warm tone of this yellow green works in harmony with the warm taupe of the hat and shawl.*

BRIGHT *Magenta and lime yellow-green make a bold color statement and are wonderful against dark skin tones. These colors translate successfully into fabrics such as linen, gauze, and silk jersey.*

MUTED *Together, warm brown and muted yellow-green are rich and elegant—especially for fall and winter wardrobes.*

Day Color

Pale YELLOW-GREENs only faintly suggest any sense of green, making the yellow tone much more prominent. A warm, beautiful color against dark skin tones, these shades are very attractive in tropical environments when used in washed silk or sheer, lightweight linens in simple, classic shapes. When translated into mohair or cashmere, this difficult color is sensual and tactile and combines well with rich suede accents.

Evening Color

As YELLOW-GREEN travels past the celadon and chartreuse of day-time, and deepens to more acid and moss green tones, it translates into choices for suits and matt jersey dressing. These unexpected interpretations of a youthful hue leave interesting visual memories about the wearer. A beautiful evening dress in an iridescent yellow-green taffeta appears elegant and aloof.

Yellow-green Textiles

YELLOW-GREEN for day wear looks rich used in fluid, matte fabrics. Considered urban and modern, and rarely produced in lace, this interesting color translates well into shiny vinyl for outerwear, fluffy fleece-wear for relaxing, and iridescent spandex for simple, glamorous gowns.

Green

Green

Green is complex; a vast palette from fresh to sophisticated.

GREEN symbolizes nature, eternal life, permanence, and value. Like bountiful gardens and groves of trees, it suggests perpetual growth and health. Long considered an "anti-fashion" color, it now reflects a near universal desire to be in harmony with nature. Both green and blue share a huge range of tints and shades, and both are identified by the same word in Japanese. Bright shades of green suggest excitement and activity, while darker shades are cool and restful.

Analogous

Deep green and navy blue work well together visually, because they are a natural progression of hues. With the lush texture of velvet added, they evoke the enchantment of a deep forest in this stylish hat for the country or city

Monochromatic

Light monochromatic color schemes can be boring without a point of contrast. Subdued and grayish, these linen shirts are distinguished by the addition of a patterned silk shawl for interest.

Complementary

Lightening complementaries to pastels softens their impact. This pink sweater becomes pale against the vivid green contrast of the sweater, but the addition of white (in the striped turtleneck) helps the balance of this scheme.

Combining Green

GREEN, the color between blue and yellow, is associated with youth, delicate new growth, coolness and nature. Green is one of the only colors that can effectively describe a

PALE *Pairing yellow and green of similar hues works best if texture is introduced for interest. In this illustration, the dress is linen and the soft cape is woven silk and linen.*

WARM *The almond green sweater enhances the bright warm tones of the yellow-orange trouser, making a lively mix for a casual outfit.*

scent. Contrasting pure green with yellow or black creates bright combinations that look sporty. Adding a measure of white or blue focuses the combination, and gives the hues more vibrance. Mint green balances well with pastels, but mixes poorly with gold, ivory, and earthy neutrals. Small amounts of turquoise green look beautiful with black or white.

COOL *Blue and green are always a strong and attractive color combination, popular in both modern and classic clothing styles.*

TRANQUIL *A pale pink skirt topped with rich green achieves harmony and balanced proportion in this scheme.*

COLD *When blue and green are equal in tone, as here, they communicate a cold feeling. Using a matte fabric distracts from this, allowing the rich saturation of color to dominate.*

DRAMATIC *Deep forest green richly accented with violet is full bodied and spirited. This noble combination is wonderful for fall or winter wardrobes.*

Day Color

The palest GREEN, almost the transparent color of soap bubbles, in linen, cotton, and floral chiffon, evokes coolness in hot, humid weather. Shades of opal and jade in cool wool and jersey fabrics work for every season. Wardrobes in a monochromatic green scheme are functional and elegant, especially when travelling through various climates where layering of clothing is convenient option.

Evening Color

Suits for fall in rich, nubby tweeds in shades of emerald and spruce are good choices for urban or country wear. And a deep hunter GREEN velvet gown worn for a formal occasion projects a magical, timeless quality about the wearer.

Green Textiles

GREEN is frequently combined with reds, blues or yellows in a foulard motif, a small-scale pattern printed by machine. The classic foulard patterns are small regular-shaped geometrics, usually produced in silk. The finished garment often is a blouse or necktie intended to be worn with a wool tweed suit.

Blue-green

Blue-green

BLUE-GREEN conjures up images of quiet and soothing tropical seas and sunlit waters. It evokes youth and energy, coolness and serenity. Blue-green is a malleable color in clothing ensembles: paired with black or strong, primary colors, it can look ethnic (think of American Indian styles such as turquoise and silver jewelry, and bold blanket patterns), with pastels it can look sweet and youthful, and in geometric patterns with bright colors it communicates a sleek, art deco message.

A perennial fashion favorite, blue-green enjoyed renewed popularity in the1980s—thanks to the collections of French designer Christian Lacroix.

Blue-green is cool and elegant.

Split-complementary

Because blue-green has a wide range, its impression changes depending on how it is worn. Used as an accent color, whether in an ensemble or an accessory, it boosts the graphic impact of strong shades of red, orange, and blue.

Analogous

Blue-green is a cool color, but because it contains some yellow undertones from its component of green, it can be worn successfully with warm hues. Here it holds it own with a deep tone and a sour shade of yellow-green.

Subdued Monochromatic

Blue-green softens and appears muted when worn with a warm neutral. Grayish tones unite this outfit, while the strong contrasts of pattern give it focus. Simple, quiet schemes like this one suggest Japanese style.

Combining Blue-green

BLUE-GREEN was at the height of its popularity in the deco fashions of the 1920s, and again in the 1930s as an accessory color for women's shoes. Popular with mature women, and

SOFT *A grayed-cactus blue-green worn over eggshell gabardine trousers, is contemporary and tropical in mood.*

COMPOSED *Adding a terra cotta shawl to this dress plays up the complementary colors and is chic without being hard-edged.*

flattering to most, it is a surprisingly strong color. It visually absorbs red, and becomes lively and electric when paired with red orange, its complement. With primary colors or black, it advances toward the viewer; with pastels, grays, or analogous tints, it recedes. Highly changeable, blue-green can suggest either slick modernity or complete naturalness, depending on the shade or tint chosen.

TROPICAL *Red violet accessorizes this seafoam strapless dress in a glamorous combination for tropical evenings.*

SUBDUED *Adding black to blue-green subdues the color, making a perfect foil for the soft gray of the shawl.*

DRAMATIC *Layers, and saturated deep color, make plum and teal rich and exotic.*

MATURE *An element of iridescence used with blue-green creates elegance.*

Day Color

Soft blue or turquoise has been popular in women's clothing since the 1920s, and in modern active wear a brighter turquoise, often combined with black, is well established. All shades of BLUE-GREEN are appropriate for day, and the color works with many styles; from a classic sweater set to wear with cool linens to a vibrant, peacock blue suede shirt dress. Whether in suits of fine lightweight wools or in nubby tweeds for cooler climates, it is a flattering color for women of all skin tones. Blue-green in all values is especially attractive with silver jewelry.

Evening Color

Mid-range sapphire BLUE-GREEN in silk pongee or fully saturated teal blue in satin are rich and elegant choices for evening wear. Because of light absorption and reflection, fabric choice is critical to wearing blue-green at night. Shiny or silky textures will intensify the color, rough weaves will deepen it, and matte or flat fabrics will alter it, making it appear more gray, black, or evergreen.

Blue-green Textiles

BLUE-GREEN has always been popular in suede, especially in California, and the American Southwest. It consistently appears at craft shows in woven coats of chenille and hats of felted wool. This popular color produced in wool tweed is a favorite for conservative city suits.

Blue

Blue

Blue is reliable and strong.

BLUE comes in a huge range of tints and shades, and is the easiest color for most people to wear. Whether light tints or dark shades of blue are coordinated, the effect is clear, cool, and defined. Blue has as many moods as the world has nationalities: it is the color of holiness for the Hebrews and the Hindus; in Japan, blue stands for spring and victory; in America and Britain blue is popular for workers clothes, whether for bankers or laborers.

The blue message varies dramatically with each deepening shade. The hush of pale blue is delicate and innocent, yet a nautical navy stings with the excitement of sailing and the salty sea air.

Primary Scheme

Blue becomes a canvas when geometric patterns of yellow, and red are applied to resemble an abstract painting. The strength of vivid blue can be overpowering when worn alone; it is best in schemes with other strong primaries (or black or white) and with simple shapes or bold pattern divisions.

Contrasting

Blue against a cool neutral is muted and modern. Sharp contrasts of blue and a neutral project a businesslike, urbane image. Though both scarf and sweaters are soft, this outfit is sharp and sophisticated.

Saturated

Visibility increases with dissimilar combinations, such as deep indigo and white. Colors of strong contrast increase the illusion of both height and width, so wearers should take care in adopting this bold look. Cold indigo and white links this coat to the traditional shapes of the Orient and the colors of Scandinavia.

Combining Blue

Most women can wear BLUE. A dark blue suit has become a basic for many wardrobes. Both pale and bright colors work well with navy. For a more contemporary combination try a mono-

PALE *The soft quality of pale blue and pink together are very flattering. These colors translate well into soft fluid fabrics such as washed silk or chiffon.*

FRESH *The contrast of cool blue and cool pink is refreshing but becomes more interesting when a third color is added in an accessory such as blue-green of the same value.*

chromatic scheme in matte jersey or wear a well-cut navy jacket over black. To balance very pale blues, use pastels or neutrals such as pale gray and white—too bright, warm colors will overwhelm pale blue. Royal blue can be used with either pastels or primary colors. The combination of royal blue and black is sophisticated but very strong—in formal styles it can appear rigid and hard.

COOL *Blue and green in clear, mid-tones and in balanced proportions create a cool impression in lightweight linens or knitwear in simple shapes.*

QUIET *Using two shades of grayish blue, one very pale, the other almost gray creates a sophisticated combination. Be sure to adjust these subdued shades to your skin tone.*

BRIGHT *Bright blue and emerald green are a hard combination. They work best when the main garment is in one color and the second color is used as an accent.*

DEEP *The richness of navy with magenta is especially luxurious when combined in wool tweed or in handknit sweaters for the country.*

Day Color

BLUE is basically cool, but it easily harmonizes with a range of colors, including most shades of green, red, and violet, and black, gray, and most neutrals. This allows great flexibility for accessories for day wear. From the palest baby blue hues in light-weight fabrics or washed denims for casual and country wear, to slate-toned flannels and classically austere navy for urban dressing, there is a shade for every wardrobe and climate. The important message is to choose the tone and fabric that best suits your lifestyle.

Evening Color

Dramatic and rich cobalt or Prussian BLUE make an easy transition into evening in suits of silk or wool crepe, while ink or midnight blue in brocades trimmed with touches of gold, or in simple shapes in velvet under a voluminous silk taffeta cape, create a dramatic unforgettable effect.

Blue Textiles

More and more designers are using top weight worsted, BLUE pin striped fabrics borrowed from menswear. Genuine indigo is made with vegetable dye instead of chemicals, which affects the way it behaves in fabric. Navy blue continues to be popular in tartans and classic cashmere.

Violet

Violet

violet is cool and unpredictable.

VIOLET looks easy, but is hard to wear. Pretty on blondes and redheads, it tends to make golden or dark complexions appear washed out. Hard to accessorize, because it is not a primary color and it bridges the gap between red and blue, violet clothing is appealing in the store but challenging once you get it home. Noble and lush, a hue once reserved for royalty, this unpredictable color evokes elements of magic and surprise. During the nineteenth century, when aniline dyes were invented, deep violet became more available. In the 1940s, Italian designer Emilio Pucci often included violet purple in his bold silk prints. Today, violet is found in many wardrobes in subdued shades of lilac and amethyst.

Monochromatic

Pale violet can seem dreamy, deepening its hue to red-violet projects sophistication. Here, adding a red-violet shawl, in a shade slightly deeper than the sweater, to a grayed-violet suit completes this controlled scheme. The black hat adds urban refinement.

contrasting

Accenting black with deep violet is authoritative. Changes from one deep, saturated color to a deeper color placed adjacent, create the powerful impression of gathering darkness. The use of silk taffeta in the scarf adds boldness and sheen to the matte black.

Accent

Violet can be slightly offbeat. Used with yellow-green or orange it becomes whimsical, even clownish. Pattern can have the same effect: dots or stripes with violet appear more whimsical. This tie combines red-violet and white to accessorize a conventional pin-striped suit, the effect indicates humor.

combining violet

Yellow, the true complement of VIOLET, balances the hue but is practically impossible to wear as a combination. Secondary colors such as orange and green are slightly easier

WARM *The subdued heather tone of the jacket is warmed by adding the red-violet scarf for an elegant cold weather combination.*

HOT *A red-violet silk sweater over the blue violet jumpsuit is vibrant, sensual and daring.*

to pair with violet, and can be worn with some success. Pink is a natural partner for very feminine looks, and ivory and cool blues enhance violet's grace and elegance. Teamed with most pastels, pale violet can act almost as a neutral. Take care with ensembles of deep gray or black with violet, if the contrast is too great the violet will appear flat and muddy.

REFINED *These slightly dull colors reflect a Japanese scheme with urban refinement.*

SUBDUED *Sweater dressing, combining slightly grayed colors that are balanced in value, evokes a country mood.*

DEFINED *Direct and uncomplicated, this combination uses magenta with black. The results are sophisticated and timeless.*

DEEP *When violet is darkened by adding black it becomes aubergine—as in this jacket; when worn with a deep green skirt of equal tone, this two-color suit is chic and feminine.*

Day Color

Pale VIOLET in floral print dresses has always been popular with older women, but new color combinations such as lavender blue with black are becoming popular with all age groups. Combining deeper shades of blue purple with brown, or plum with hunter green, looks rich and urban and translates well in fabrics such as wool knits and gabardine.

Evening Color

Purple in varied dark tones in light chiffon, sheer stripes, or ethnic patterned gauzes is sophisticated for evening in warm climates; for cool climates, rich silk jersey in aubergine or deep VIOLET stretch satin, or plisse in simple silhouettes are noble statements for this regal color.

Violet Textiles

VIOLET dye was first discovered in the Bronze Age, several hundreds of years before the Mediterranean trade in the Phoenicians' Tyrian purple, and was one of the first to be synthesized. Often referred to as plum or aubergine, this royal color is beautiful when produced in pleated silk pongee or silk seersucker.

Pink

Pink

Pretty in PINK is the ultimate cliche, but actually looking pretty in pink is more difficult than it seems. Local light has a lot to do with it; pink can go from fragile to washed-out looking very easily. It's a coquettish color with its own personality, quite distinct from its cousin color red. Long associated with sweetness, youth, and innocence, pink is really a chameleon: this perennial favorite is popular for both men and women in traditional Indian textiles, shocking in the fashion vogue of the 1930s (after designer Elsa Schiaparelli introduced a saturated, sizzling version of the color in the United States), and modern and far-from-pastel during the pyrotechnics of the 1960s in Europe and North America.

Pink is a tough color with a sweet reputation.

Complementary

Light pink looks tropical in combination with emerald green. This mix is cool, not only because it evokes the colors of a freshly cut watermelon, but because pale pinks contain a large amount of white, which lightens them and partially blocks the warm end of the spectrum of light, enhancing cool tones.

Monochromatic

Pink is actually a tint of red, the result of adding white to the base color. Though monochromatic in tone, this simple color combination of pink and red hues looks spirited and theatrical. The dullness of the suede against the shine of satin ribbons enhances the subtle differences in hue.

Tone on Tone

A large field of pink can look somewhat indistinct. Adding small amounts of a very dark tone, such as the black flecks and plaid collar shown here, helps to anchor and punctuate the shade. This splash of strong contrast brings an air of elegance and polish to an otherwise ethereal color.

Combining Pink

PINK runs the gamut from baby pink to fuchsia in its most saturated form. Worn alone, pink can easily become overpowering. It seems to work best

PALE *Pale pink with mint in linen or silk is a popular summer combination, and is especially attractive on light complexions and with gray or silver hair.*

WARM *A fuchsia wool jacket worn with a matching gabardine skirt adds a bright bolt of color for evenings during the winter. Adding the cool green knit vest sharpens the intensity of fuchsia.*

worn with pure colors, rather than colors shaded with brown or black, but there are no hard and fast rules for combining pink. Oriental artists historically have mixed pink and red. In the 1950s and 1960s, designers in the West even started combining pink with orange to make bold and electric collections.

SOFT *Pale pink and pale blue work well together. Combining very pale and soft colors is easy, since paleness makes the area where two colors meet less distinct.*

TRANQUIL *The soft tones of beige and frosted pink are similar in value and, when clearly defined, create a natural, gentle, but chic combination.*

BRILLIANT *Combining bright tones with deep ones frames the brighter color the way darkness frames a lighted window. Bright pink with deep blue-purple emphasizes the brilliance of the pink.*

STRIKING *Magenta with red-orange is unexpected. This combination's strength can stand up to harsh light, and looks beautiful against tanned or dark skin.*

Day Color

PINK is hardest to wear in strong daylight, unless it is very saturated or accented with deep tones. Soft tints of pink are flattering to most women, but again, local light is a factor, as well as skin tone. The addition of white to pastel combinations of pink sharpens the contrast of the pastels and brings them into focus. As a main color, pink often conveys an impression of sweetness or cuteness. This can be used to advantage as a counterpoint in styles with a serious nature or severe cut.

Evening Color

The drama of PINK is expressed as it approaches fuchsia or magenta. The elegance of these evening shades is best translated using shantung silks that add an additional range of surface color due to the shiny texture of this exotic fabric. The traditional association between pink and romance strengthens its cachet as a color for evening dress.

pink Textiles

William Henry Hoffman discovered the aniline dye called magenta, named after a battle fought in northern Italy in 1859. Paler shades of magenta—PINK and rose—are commonly found in circle or dot motifs, the most common geometric pattern on printed cloth. Pinks—worked tonally into stepweave tweeds and high-twist yarns—are important new looks for career and casual wear.

Neutrals

Neutrals

NEUTRAL colors blend effortlessly. Peaceful and warm, their monochromatic palette is pure and modest, like unbleached cotton, pale linen or rough textured wool, they are natural and simple. Their classic look suggests a sense of elegance, of summer's answer to black, but neutrals can also provide a canvas for a dramatic burst of color. This not only changes the mood but also shows the versatility of neutrals.

Neutrals are quiet
and reassuring,
timeless and elegant.

Monochromatic

The woven linen suit and white sweater create a neutral background for the volume of the necklace. The scheme is quiet and tactile.

Primary with Neutral

The red sweater against the two neutrals in this outfit adds a rakish dash of warmth and color.

contrast

This subdued combination employs light-flecked dark tones that enhance texture.

Combining Neutrals

NEUTRALS are muted versions of saturated colors, therefore, the underlying color must be identified. For example, yellow green, or pink

TRANQUIL *Strong and classic, both jacket and skirt hues have been grayed in this outfit to create a harmonious mood.*

ELEGANT *The green has been neutralized in this cool, almost chilly, combination. The deeper tone of the coat gives strength to this elegant winter outfit.*

can be lightened or subdued without losing the color. Tan is light brown. White or beige consistently mix well with other colors or shades. Often a neutral color scheme is referred to as Japanese style, or *shibui,* because of its natural, muted feeling.

WARM *A mushroom-toned coat emphasizes the warmth of the brown scarf and hat for a refined and chic message.*

DULL *A brighter hue is introduced in the lining, cuff and pocket design and enhances this subdued greige coat.*

CONTRAST *Yellow-based neutral, a hue that suggests natural linen, works well with the coffee-tones of a turtleneck sweater.*

EARTHY *These warm, red-based hues suggest ginger and aubergine for a carefully balanced combination that is rich with artistic style.*

Day Color

The pale NEUTRAL palette includes many tints, from misty green gray, yellowish beige, to grayed browns; all are excellent choices for both casual and business dress. They also translate well to textured fabrics, linens, and cool wools, and span many climates and occasions. Natural colors are harmonious and easy to combine even when using shades of one hue.

Evening Color

As NEUTRALS move to evening and soft mid-tone, the beige deepens to cinnamon, the gray becomes smoky, and brown becomes mocha.

This quiet palette works in delicate fabrics, like georgette and velvet, or the newer blended acrylics and in cashmere and silk.

Neutral Textiles

Prized for their warmth, comfort, and softness, natural materials come with their own, ready-made palette of colors. Long before the advent of dyes, noble fibers such as cashmere, baby alpaca, wools, silk, and mohair have dictated a neutral palette of colors for cool weather. In warm climates, the textured weaves of cottons, knits, sheer linens, and silks are used to give weight to those fabrics' light colors when they are used in their natural state.

Black

Black

Throughout history BLACK was associated with dark and somber occasions implying mystery and corruption. It is, however, a forceful color in fashion. As a basic it takes on a role similar to white as a palette for accessorizing. Black brings the focus to the wearer, as opposed to the details of the garment. Silhouette and form are a crucial part of fashion, and of wearing this color successfully. Black leather jackets have become as universal as the Gap T-shirt. Coco Chanel, the French designer, introduced "the little black dress" in the 1930s and made it famous.

Black is the monarch of the fashion world.

Ethnic Influences

Primary yellow wooden bracelets against an African shawl send a different message about black and white.

Vivid Contrast

Wrapping a simple black dress in a bold colored shawl has a strong and festive effect.

Exotic

A simple black coat trimmed in an exotic faux fur provides a strong color accent.

Combining Black

BLACK has dominated fashion perhaps more than any color other than red. When in doubt, wear

WARM *A skirt in medium red orange brings warmth to the charcoal black blouse and three-quarter-length black coat.*

SUBDUED *Introducing a rich subdued red punctuates the low contrast of a charcoal and black knit outfit.*

black. A practical solution to every woman's fashion dilemma. Black is a perfect canvas for accent color and allows the wearer to make the outfit suit their own personality.

COLD *Gray offers a contrast in brightness to the black coat. The yellow-green suede bag gives the outfit a modern accent.*

MODERN *Pale yellow, the color of cornsilk, is sensitive and modern with the black suit.*

MUTED *Texture is introduced for contrast and interest in a gray jacket worn over a black dress. The rich teal scarf adds a stylish dash of color.*

DRAMATIC *The ocher dress under the black coat illustrates how a concentrated color is enhanced when paired with black. Matte jersey, linen, or cool wool are good fabric choices for these simple shapes.*

Day Color

BLACK, a mysterious color, can emphasize the brilliance of any color with which it is combined. Just as white suggests innocence, black evokes sophistication. There are green blacks, blue blacks, brown blacks, etc. The underlying color should be carefully identified before adding an accent color. Black runs the gamut in shape and fabric, from activewear in Lycra, flannel, and sweatshirting, to professional dress in cool linens, gabardines and knits.

Evening color

The little BLACK dress, Victorian shapes in black lace, caftans in silk chiffon, a velvet evening jacket embellished with jet beads, or a dramatic brocade cape over a ball-gown, black for evening is universal and socially correct.

Black Textiles

Texture, drape, shine, mini-herringbones and chevrons. BLACK is the core of the wardrobe, it is where it all begins. Black fabrics can be successfully beaded, embroidered, pleated and crinkled, or embellished. Light weight and high sheen fabrics will rob black of some of its depth; compared to velvet, which accepts full saturation. It is important to match blacks in daylight, as artificial light can distort the color. Every season new colors are introduced by designers and editorialized in the fashion press. But no one ever abandons black, and when you look around a room full of fashion editors, they are all wearing black!

White

White

white is aristocratic and refined.

WHITE is a chameleon, sensitive to every hue. By absorbing the palest tints it becomes soft and romantic. From creamy ivory to cool parchment tones, white lends itself to more basic and coarse executions. Wovens and transparent fabrics add to white's flexible attributes. With layers of winter white wool, or clouds of transparent white voile and gauze, white creates a mood of daydreaming, of simple freedom. White transcends the fickleness of fashion with its elegance, purity, and honesty. It is easy to use as both foundation and accent, and in combination with other colors.

Contrasting

A jacket in a bold weave of black against white makes such a strong statement that it requires no jewelry.

Balanced

Tone is important when combining white with a neutral, as in the subdued taupe blouse. The scheme then maintains composure and elegance.

Warm

Adding the sweater vest of red-orange to the white blouse suggests a sporty, casual mood.

combining white

WHITE has interesting qualities related to color and texture. White on white in a monochromatic

PALE *The effect of the slight tint in the stripe gives the fabric a feeling of transparency in this sedate summer suit.*

BRIGHT *A chalk white jacket brightens the red orange of the skirt for a refreshing sporty statement.*

scheme is powerful and sophisticated, and with black, timeless. It absorbs powdery tints of grey, pink, lavender, and blue. A perennial fashion favorite, it remains a symbol of elegance.

NATURAL *The neutral tint of the skirt is a subdued contrast to the white blouse.*

CASUAL *Weekend separates unite with a casual, blue vest worn over shades of white.*

CLASSIC *Brown accessories introduce the classic, "spectator style" when worn with a white suit.*

COOL *A voluminous, porcelain white blouse works to balance a the narrow teal suede skirt.*

Day Color

WHITE is a summer essential any way you wear it. From the universal T-shirt to simple sundresses, white pants, white shorts, or big shirts. Like black, white serves as a wardrobe foundation and essential.

Evening Color

Impeccable WHITE suits, bare silk dresses for tropical evenings, diaphanous whites for a candle lit evening, white Lycra for glamour. White needs no passport, it transcends all cultures and seasons with timeless elegance.

White Textiles

White has its own palette; natural chalk is opaque white, eggshells are a translucent, off-white, zinc is a brilliant, blue-white or yellow-white. All appear white except when placed side by side. In fabric it is much the same: White mohair is a different color white than white linen, just by the nature of the fibers. Lace, crochet, or any open weave also changes the color of white.

Gray

Gray

The hard edge and strength of GRAY combines with a sense of permanence: for not only does gray provide the foundation in our architecture, it can also provide the foundation for our wardrobes. The color gray suggests confidence, like a gray flannel suit. It implies permanence and bestows a sense of sophistication and savoir faire on those who wear it. Gray is investment dressing. Its characteristics are subtle and lasting. Gray has a rarefied dignity, one of establishment and elegance. This neutral color is a perfect backdrop for dramatic colors such as yellow green, red, or magenta, for a less conventional and unexpected impact.

Gray is dignified and confident.

Warm

A textured monochromatic gray chenille scarf with the warm red-violet sweater is a charming and refined combination.

Contrasting

Cool yellow-green gives the medium hue gray sweater a bright, sophisticated, modern appeal.

Bright with Subdued

The use of bright red-violet as an accessory to the subdued gray gives this outfit a fun and lively focus.

combining Gray

Conventional GRAY is associated with professional dress, it implies seriousness and hard work. A combination of black and white, gray can

PALE *Subdued green gray combined with a slightly bright white green keeps this combination from becoming melancholy.*

BALANCED *Charcoal gray with green that has been shaded by adding black gives balance to this conservative combination.*

be ambiguous and unassuming. The message can be changed when gray is used in soft fluid knits, in subdued tones that reflect fog and twilight; when layered for warmth and texture, this quiet combination is fashionable and intelligent.

SOFT *Red-violet tinted with white gives this misty gray a powdery look.*

COOL *Deep, blue gray and a pale, blue violet combined are wonderful and cool.*

DEEP *Because this combination of blue violet and medium gray is balanced, it seems to cast a faint glow.*

MUTED *Intriguing and compelling, this combination of low grayish tones works well applied to rough textures.*

Day Color

GRAY is neither black nor white but a combination of the two. In its palest form, it can be a pearl gray; as it moves towards white, it is more innocent, subtle, and refined. The power of gray for daytime is its range of moods.

Evening Color

As GRAY moves closer to black it becomes stronger, dominant, and steely. Tones of gray mixed with brown in classic-inspired tweeds can be softened with blouses of silk crepe, or pastoral chiffon prints. A simple evening dress in pewter silk velvet is modern, sophisticated, and timeless.

Gray Textiles

During the 1600s, the Japanese artist Senno Rikyu introduced a neutral hue that came to be known as *Rikyu gray.* This popular color was soon joined by silver gray, indigo gray, brown gray and dove gray, all shades of low color saturation. These grays became the hallmark of aesthetic sensibility during the Genroku era (1688-1704). They continue to be a color baseline for gray textiles in fashion today. Chenille, boucle, and tweeds, combine these tones to create interesting patterns in knitwear.

Trends

Trends

Freedom to express yourself transcends all the rules.

One of the most consistent trends in fashion and color is the use of basics. Whether they are a T-shirt and jeans or a little black dress, basics are the foundation of most wardrobes the world over. Color has also become a tool in creating a solid base for a wardrobe. With the unquestionable success of retailers like the Gap, more and more companies are following this lead and providing core garments in a range of colors that lend themselves to mixing and accessorizing. This freedom to express yourself transcends all the rules. Individuals are wearing daytime staples with evening pieces for any number of occasions. As women have become more independent they have been able to choose the kind of image they wish to project.

classics

This new confidence coupled with changes in lifestyles (less time to shop) has women choosing wardrobes of season-less classics. Uncomplicated shapes in new fabrics are softly structured, with the emphasis on textures and surface dimension. New materials are giving the classics universal appeal, as well as extended versatility and polish.

Classic shapes work well with monochromatic color schemes. Mixing tweeds with silk shirts and adding a beautifully constructed big coat, made with new combinations of acetate and wool, offers both lightness of weight and extended wearability.

Women want to put quality and performance back into their wardrobes, without sacrificing sophisticated fashion.

Knitwear & Leisure

Throughout the world, lifestyles have changed to reflect a more relaxed attitude; businesses have incorporated casual days for workers, and new, lighter and wrinkle-free fabrics comfortably travel into many different climates.

Knitwear is emerging as a wardrobe essential. Women can build a knitwear wardrobe of simple, mix-and-match pieces by coordinating both silhouette and color. New technology in knitwear allows for dramatic applications of color. Knits work well because they can be layered for travel, are always comfortable and are compact.

Cashmere, mohair, and wool chenille are newly popular, as are sleek acetate knits with the hand of silk. Some of the newest fabrics now available mix manmade fibers with natural elements, a development reflected in casual and leisure clothing. Exciting yarn mixes, strong colorations, easy care, and a relaxed attitude are the current criteria for fabrics—as witnessed in the popularity of fleece, stretch jersey and textured knitwear.

Denim & Outerwear

Denim continues to be important. Universally understood and accepted in its original blue, denim has recently become sophisticated in deep saturated hues of blackened brown, carbon paper blue, and forest green.

Wrap coats and trench coats are entering the twenty-first century in shiny reflective textures, embossed reptile skins, and rubbery leathers. Outerwear is becoming more versatile, moving from day to evening in easy-care synthetics of silky jersey. Camel, gray and red are adjusting to different levels of saturation and interpretation but continue to remain color classics. Black still maintains an authority of universal style.

Basic Black

The move toward sensible clothes represents a trend toward quality and good design in building a functional wardrobe. Clean, well-cut classics are becoming the foundation for a woman's wardrobe. These are clothes worth investing in and building on. Silhouettes that are versatile are important. The key is shape. A carefully chosen, simple black dress can work for day or evening. A bright, colorful jacket enhances a simple wool dress. Black is a canvas. Black invites individual interpretation.

Some of the most beautiful accessories are simple, non-commercial items crafted for galleries. They range from jewel-toned Fortuny evening bags to exquisite scarves, with iridescent hems, or whimsical pastel patterns painted on sheer silk.

Dark velvets, rich stained-glass colors in tapestry and jacquard fabrics borrowed from home furnishings translate well into beautiful evening jackets to wear over a simple black velvet evening dress.

Timeless design is still, however, basic black—now and historically, the most important fashion statement.

About the Author

Mary Garthe is principal of *Mary Garthe Associates,* a fashion consulting group in Boston, Massachusetts. She advises clients in styling photo shoots, planning product line fashion presentations, apparel studies and craft seminars. Her clients include *Laura Ashley USA, Keds,* and the Canadian Consulate General, Boston. Ms. Garthe has done cover shoots or styling for several Boston magazines including *Design Times, Boston* magazine, and *Maverick Magazine.* Prior to starting her consulting business, Ms. Garthe was the Regional Director of the *Fashion Group International/Boston* and owned a women's specialty store on Boston's North Shore. Ms. Garthe was honored as the 1992 "Woman of the Year" by the Retail Management Program at Lasell College.

About the Photographer

John Kane, the owner of *Silver Sun Studios,* lives and works in Litchfield County, Connecticut with his wife Wendy Carlson. In addition to fashion, he also photographs dance, and has had many corporate and advertising assignments. His work has been published in magazines all over the world.

About the Illustrator

Michael Lenn (Misha) is a freelance fashion illustrator, graphic designer, and fine artist. His clients include *Sony, The New York Times, Filene's* Boston, *Bloomingdales, Houghton Mifflin Company* and *Heinle & Heinle Publishers.* Misha is a native of St. Petersburg, Russia. He received his B.A. in 1982 and M.A. in 1984 from Mukhina's College of Art and Design, St. Petersburg, Russia.

contributor credits

RED

Page 12-13, Red cashmere suit, Bloomingdales, Chestnut Hill, MA
Model: Juenelle, Maggie, Inc. Boston

Page 14, Red mohair coat, ŌKẄ, Boston, black velvet hat, Bloomingdales, Chestnut Hill, MA
Location: Stillington Hall, Gloucester, MA
Model: Liz Vago, Maggie, Inc. Boston

Page 15, top, Red leather boot, Cuoio, Boston
Page 15, center, Red sweater, Bloomingdales, Chestnut Hill, MA, wool scarf, Signature Gallery, Chestnut Hill, Boston
Model: Christine Clemente, Maggie, Inc. Boston
Page 15, bottom, Red, orange sweaters, denim jumper, Lord & Taylor
Model: Katrice Navarra, Independent

Page 20-21, photography, Art of Light

ORANGE

Page 22-23, Coat, Henri Bendel
Model: Dalarna, Copley Seven, Boston

Page 24, Coat, Henri Bendel
Model: Dalarna, Copley Seven, Boston

Page 25, top, Hat, Henri Bendel
Page 25, center, Brown wool dress, Eileen Fisher, Boston, necklaces courtesy Mary Garthe
Model: Dalarna, Copley Seven, Boston
Page 25, bottom, Coat, Henri Bendel, brown suede shoes, Filene's, Boston

Page 30-31, photography, Art of Light

YELLOW

Page 32-33, Yellow coat, Bloomingdales, Chestnut Hill, Boston
Model: Juenelle, Maggie, Inc. Boston

Page 34, Yellow jacket, stripe sweater, Kirsten Scarcelli, NYC/Maine, hat, Ann Taylor, Boston
Model: Shawna Cornelius, Copley Seven, Boston

Page 35, top, Yellow fleece jacket, vest, Henri Bendel
Model: Dalarna, Copley Seven, Boston
Page 35, center, Yellow silk blouse, scarf, Alfred Fiandaca, Boston
Model: Liz Vago, Maggie, Inc. Boston
Page 35, bottom, Multi colored vest, MEH, Copley Place, shirt, The Gap
Model: Christine Clemente, Maggie, Inc. Boston

Page 40-41, photography, Art of Light

YELLOW-GREEN

Page 42-43, Jacket, sweater, pants, Henri Bendel
Model: Dalarna, Copley Seven, Boston

Page 44, Jacket, sweater, Henri Bendel

Model: Dalarna, Copley Seven, Boston

Page 45, top, Jacket, sweater, beret, Filene's, Boston
Model: Katrice Navarra, Independent
Page 45, center, Sweater, vest, Henri Bendel
Model: Dalarna, Copley Seven, Boston
Page, 45, bottom, Chenille sweater and vest, silk scarf, Lord & Taylor
Model: Marlana Cole, Independent

Page 50-51, photography, Art of Light

GREEN

Page 52-53, Green dress, Alfred Fiandaca, Boston
Location: Eliot Hotel, Boston
Model: Dalarna, Copley Seven, Boston

Page 54, Sweaters, Kirsten Scarcelli, NYC/Maine, hat, Ann Taylor, Boston
Model: Shawna Cornelius, Copley Seven, Boston

Page 55, top, Velvet hat, Cuoio, Boston, sweater, Kirsten Scarcelli, NYC/Maine
Model: Juenelle, Maggie, Inc. Boston
Page 55, center, Silk jacket, shirt, Flatiron Workshop NYC, scarf courtesy Catharine Arnston
Model: Christine Clemente, Maggie, Inc. Boston
Page 55, bottom, Sweaters, Filene's, Boston
Model: Shawna Cornelius, Copley Seven, Boston

Page 60-61, photography, Art of Light

BLUE-GREEN

Page 62-63, Dress, Kirsten Scarcelli, NYC/Maine, hat, shoes, Ann Taylor, Boston
Location: Black Falcon Cruise Terminal, courtesy of MASSPORT Boston
Model: Shawna Cornelius, Copley Seven, Boston

Page 64, Sweater, Kirsten Scarcelli, NYC/Maine
Model: Shawna Cornelius, Copley Seven, Boston

Page 65, top, Blanket bag, Pendleton Shop, Boston
Model: Marlana Cole, Independent
Page 65, center, Ruffle neck silk tee shirts, Flatiron Workshop, NYC
Model: Katrice Navarra, Independent
Page 65, bottom, Silk sweaters, scarf Filene's, Boston
Model: Marlana Cole, Independent

Page 70-71, photography, Art of Light

BLUE

Page 72-73, Wool coat, Alfred Fiandaca, Boston
Model: Liz Vago, Maggie, Inc. Boston

Page 74, Blue hat, Louis Boston
Model: Shawna Cornelius, Copley Seven, Boston

Page 75, top, Wool coat, Alfred Fiandaca, Boston
Model: Liz Vago, Maggie, Inc. Boston

Page 75, center, Sweaters, scarf, Bloomingdales, Chestnut Hill, Boston
Model: Christine Clemente, Maggie, Inc. Boston
Page 75, bottom, Indigo print coat, Anokhi, Boston, Cambridge, MA
Model: Wendy Carlson, Independent

Page 80-81, photography, Art of Light

VIOLET

Page 82-83, Velvet suit, silk blouse, Bloomingdales, Chestnut Hill, MA
Model: Juenelle, Maggie, Inc. Boston

Page 84, Model: Wendy Carlson, Independent

Page 85, top, Shawl, suit, hat, Louis Boston
Model: Dalarna, Copley Seven, Boston
Page 85, center, Black wool jacket, ŌKŴ, Boston, scarf courtesy Catharine Arnston
Page 85, bottom, Suit, shirt, tie, Louis Boston
Model: Shawna Cornelius, Copley Seven, Boston

Page 90-91, photography, Art of Light

PINK

Page 92-93, Pink dress, Laura Ashley, Boston, pink, green scarves, Bloomingdales, Chestnut Hill, MA
Boat: 1965 Riva Ariston, courtesy Nicholas Mango, Marblehead, MA
Model: Juenelle, Maggie, Inc. Boston

Page 94, Pink tweed jacket, Alfred Fiandaca, Boston
Model: Dalarna, Copley Seven, Boston

Page 95, top, pink and green scarves, Bloomingdales, Chestnut Hill, MA
Model: Juenelle, Maggie, Inc. Boston
Page 95, center, Suede shoes, Cuoio, Boston
Page 95, bottom, Pink wool crepe jacket, ŌKŴ, Boston, black velvet hat, Cuoio, Boston
Model: Juenelle, Maggie, Inc. Boston

Page 100-101, photography, Art of Light

NEUTRALS

Page 102-103, Cashmere sweaters, pants, Bloomingdales, Chestnut Hill, MA
Model: *(left)* Christine Clemente, *(right)* Juenelle, Maggie, Inc. Boston

Page 104, Suit, blouse, scarf, Laura Ashley, Boston
Model: Liz Vago, Maggie, Inc. Boston

Page 105, top, Linen suit, Rae Brewer, Boston, necklace courtesy Mary Garthe
Model: Marlana Cole, Independent
Page 105, center, Cashmere sweaters, pant, Bloomingdales, Chestnut Hill, MA
Model: Juenelle, Maggie, Inc. Boston
Page 105, bottom, Tweed sweater, Kirsten Scarcelli, NYC/Maine, bag, Cole Haan, Boston, beret, Bloomingdales, Chestnut Hill, MA
Model: Marlana Cole, Independent

Page 110-111, photography, Art of Light

BLACK

Page 112-113, (left) Black wool dress, Filene's, Boston, *(right)* Black wool dress, Eileen Fisher, Boston, Hand-painted velvet beret, Emma Gaggio, Quadrum Gallery, Boston, Chestnut Hill, MA
Model: *(left)* Juenelle, Maggie, Inc. Boston, *(right)* Dalarna, Copley Seven, Boston

Page 114, Embroidered shawl, Bloomingdales, Chestnut Hill, MA
Location: Stillington Hall, Gloucester, MA
Model: Juenelle, Maggie, Inc. Boston

Page 115, top, Shawl, bracelets, MEH Haute Couture African, Copley Place, Boston
Page 115, center, Silk taffeta shawl, courtesy Catharine Arnston
Page 115, bottom, Leopard collar jacket, Ralph Lauren, Bloomingdales, Chestnut Hill, MA
Model: Juenelle, Maggie, Inc. Boston

Page 120-121, photography, Art of Light

WHITE

Page 122-123, White pant suit, Alfred Fiandaca, Boston
Model: Juenelle, Maggie, Inc. Boston

Page 124, Model: Chris Cox, Independent

Page 125, top, Black and white wool jacket, Fiandaca, Boston
Model: Juenelle, Maggie, Inc. Boston
Page 125, center, Suit, shirt, hat, Ann Taylor, Boston
Model: Shawna Cornelius, Copley Seven, Boston
Page 125, bottom, White shirt and pant, red vest, Ann Taylor, Boston
Model: Shawna Cornelius, Copley Seven, Boston

Page 130-131, photography, Art of Light

GRAY

Page 132-133, Sweater set, pants Henri Bendel
Location: Courtesy of Patricia Fontecchio, Grange Furniture, Inc. Boston Design Center
Model: Dalarna, Copley Seven, Boston

Page 134, Sweater, chenille scarf, Henri Bendel
Model: Dalarna, Copley Seven, Boston

Page 135, top, Raspberry sweater, chenille scarf, Henri Bendel
Model: Dalarna, Copley Seven, Boston
Page 135, center, Gray sweater, green vest, Henri Bendel
Model: Dalarna, Copley Seven, Boston
Page 135, bottom, Cashmere shawl, Henri Bendel, hose by Hue, suede shoe, YSL

OTHER CREDITS

Page 6, Tweed sweater, pants, scarf, Laura Ashley, Boston
Model: Liz Vago, Maggie, Inc. Boston

Page 142, Clothing, Ann Taylor
Model: Shawna Cornelius, Copley Seven, Boston

Page 144, Suit Laura Ashley, Boston
Model: Liz Vago, Maggie, Inc. Boston

Page 145, Tweed sweater, pants, scarf, Laura Ashley, Boston
Model: Liz Vago, Maggie, Inc. Boston

Page 147, Sweater, Bloomingdales, Chestnut Hill, MA, necklace courtesy Mary Garthe
Model: Liz Vago, Maggie, Inc. Boston

Page 147, Dress, Betsy Jennings, Boston, Brookline
Model: Katrice Navarra, Independent

Page 148, Denim shirt, hat, gloves, The Gap, backpack, Cole Haan, Boston
Model: Malarna Cole

Page 149, Red mohair coat, ŌKẄ Boston, velvet hat Bloomingdales Chestnut Hill, MA
Model: Liz Vago, Maggie, Inc. Boston

Page 149, Yellow jacket, Laura Ashley, Boston
Model: Christine Clemente, Maggie, Inc. Boston
Page 151, Carrot scarf, Carol Motty, Quadrum Gallery, Boston, Chestnut Hill, MA
Model: Dalarna, Copley Seven, Boston

Page 151, Black crinkle velvet dress, The Gap
Model: Wendy Carlson, Independent
Textiles courtesy of ŌKẄ, Alfred Fiandaca, the Fabric Place, Flatiron Workshop, and George's Textiles.